DANCING on

BOOK 1

10 Early Intermediate Piano Solos

UK Exam Grade 2

CATHERINE ROLLIN

As a composer, pianist, teacher and clinician, I have learned during my travels that arts such as music and dance are languages that know no barriers or boundaries from state to state or country to country. When I was in Japan, I had the joy of hearing teachers and students play my music with great sensitivity and understanding. At one lovely party that was held in my honor, two teachers played my duet, *Polka Party*, from *Dances for Two*, Book 2. As they played, I grabbed a partner and taught her how to dance the polka right on the spot! Soon, the whole room was filled with dancing couples! What a joyous experience it was to see about 50 Japanese teachers dancing to a Polish-inspired polka, written by an American composer who only knew about five words in Japanese and none in Polish! But the language of music and dance was universal for all of us!

With *Dancing on the Keys*, Book 1, I hope that students and teachers will experience similarly the international language of music and inspire those around them to get up and dance! To these newly composed pieces, I have added a revised version of *Tap Time*, one of my first published works. I have updated the jazzy rhythms, changed a few harmonies and added an optional tapping part. In addition, several pieces have optional percussion parts indicated for more rhythmic fun!

With the advent of television shows like *Dancing with the Stars*, the joy of dancing has reached more people than in any other time in history. It is my hope that with these pieces, students and teachers will feel the rhythmic energy of the music as they literally—and figuratively—dance on the keys!

Catherine Rollin

Contents

Alfred

ISBN-10: 0-7390-4832-5
ISBN-13: 978-0-7390-4832-0

For the late Bernard Rollin, who imparted to me his love of tango, music and life.

TANTALIZING TANGO

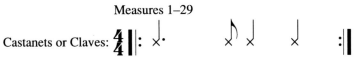

Optional Percussion:

Measures 1–29

Catherine Rollin

Moderately and dramatically

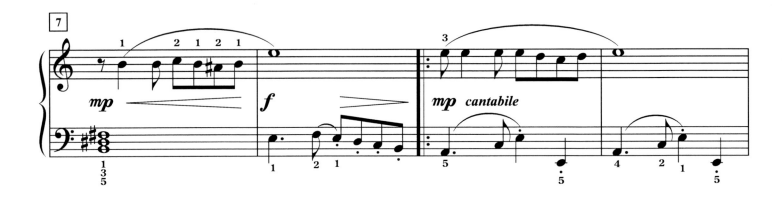

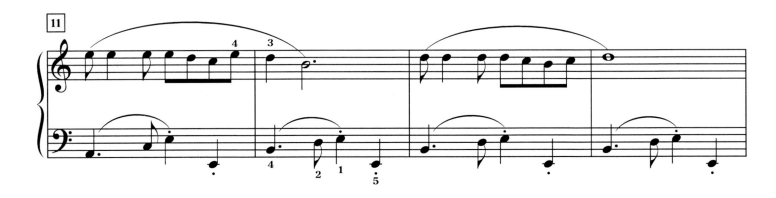

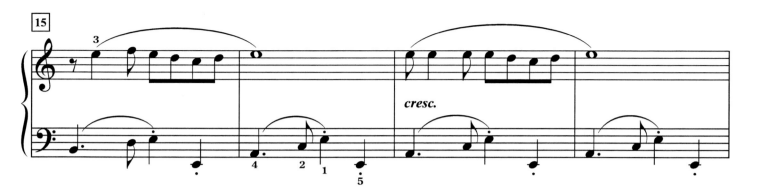

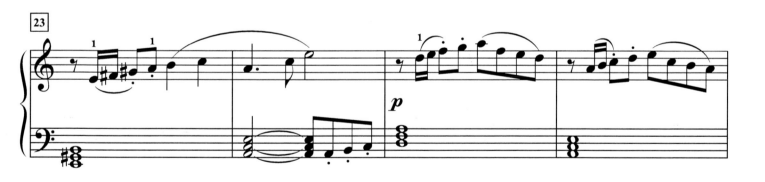

Measure 30:

For Betty Handleman Stoloff, a treasured friend whose love of music
and dedication to piano teaching are boundless and inspirational.

CONGA, CONGA, CONGA

Catherine Rollin

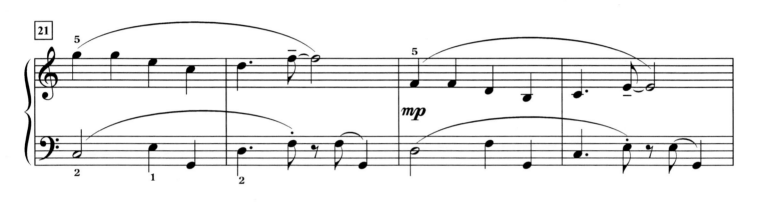

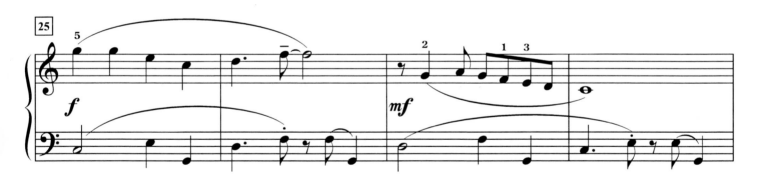

Measures 31–32

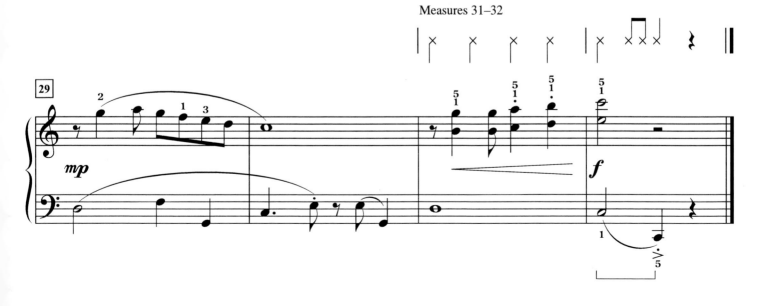

*For Jim Schnaars: Thank you for your friendship and dedication to
keeping the memory and music of Lynn Freeman Olson alive.*

TAP TIME ENCORE

Catherine Rollin

* Tap on knees or fallboard as indicated.

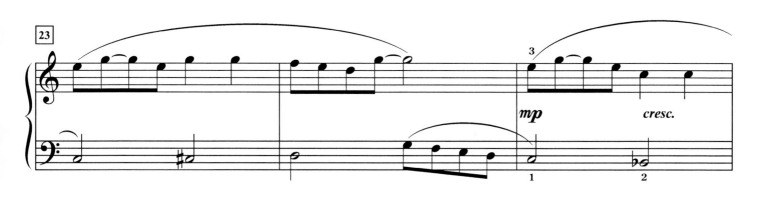

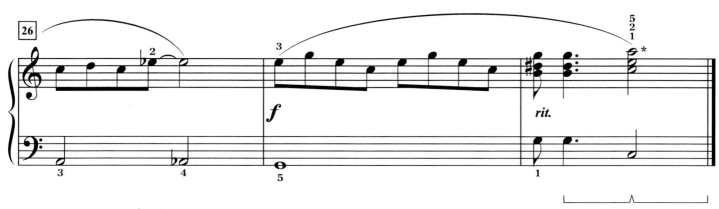

* optional tremolo:

For Albert Burke, with love.
Your enthusiasm for life is motivational and inspirational!

THE JESTER'S GIGUE

Catherine Rollin

A little more lively

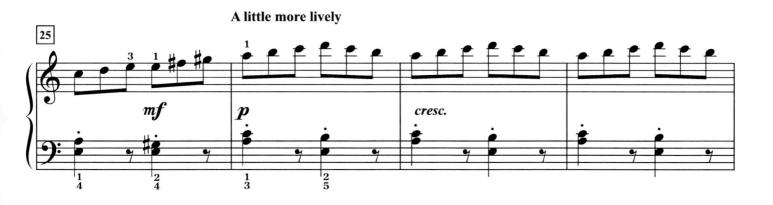

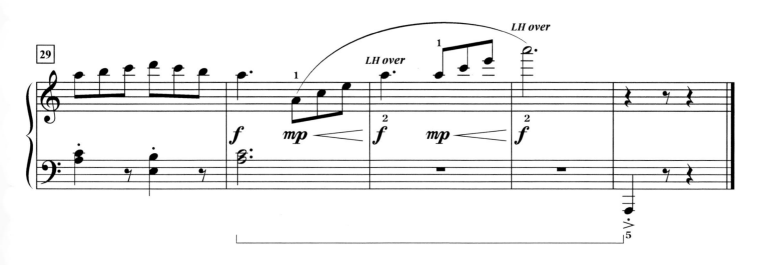

For the members of the Gillock Association of Japan:
Thank you for bringing my music to life.

ISLAND RUMBA

Catherine Rollin

* Finger pedal is suggested for the LH in measures 1–2, 13–15 and 17–19.

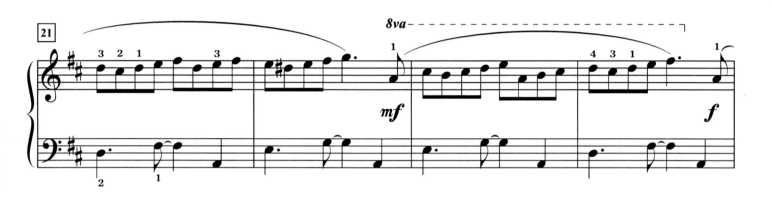

Measure 32

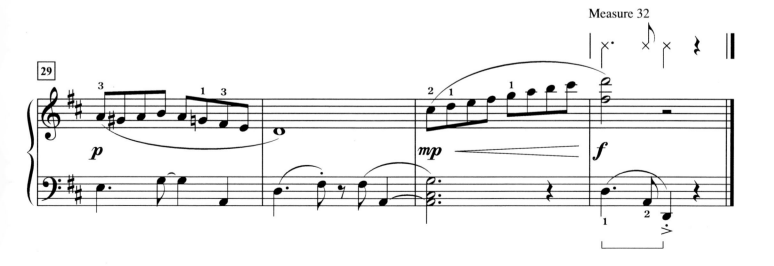

For my student, Ayaka Kimura:
Wishing you a lifetime of rewarding musical experiences.

MAZURKA FOR CHOPIN

Catherine Rollin

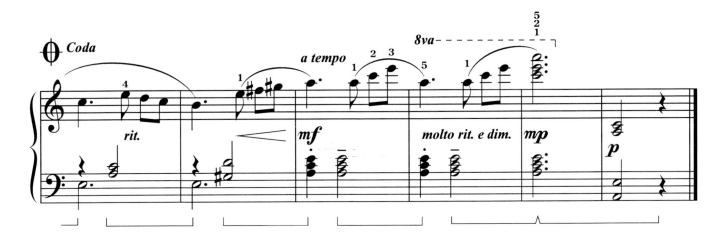

*For Hiroko Yasuda, a very special friend, with whom I have made
some of my most important musical and life journeys.*

ROCK AND ROLL SLOW DANCE

Optional Percussion:

Measures 1–26

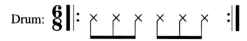

Measures 1–26

Catherine Rollin

With a strict rock beat

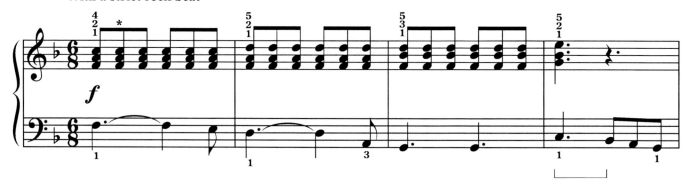

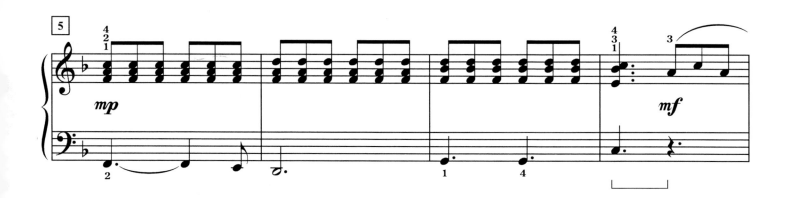

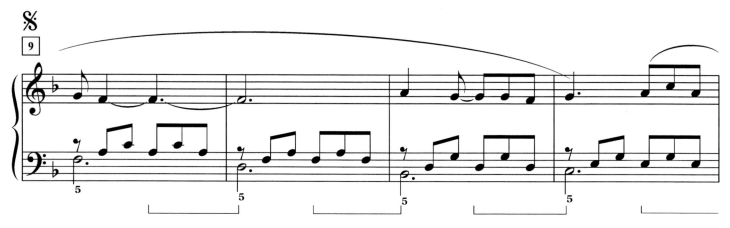

* Play the repeated chords with a *portato* touch.

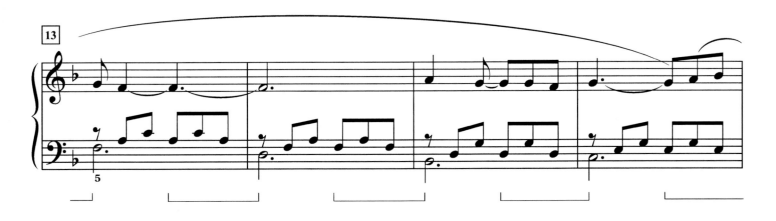

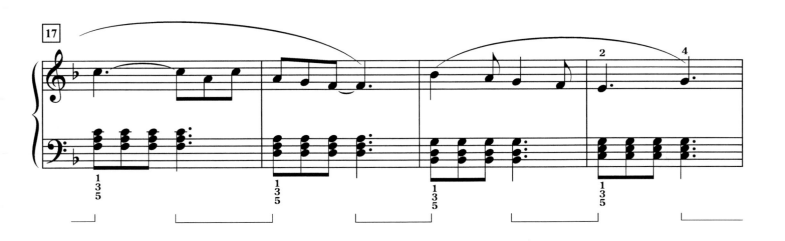

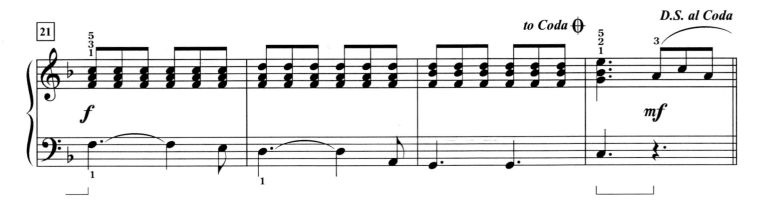

Measures 27–28

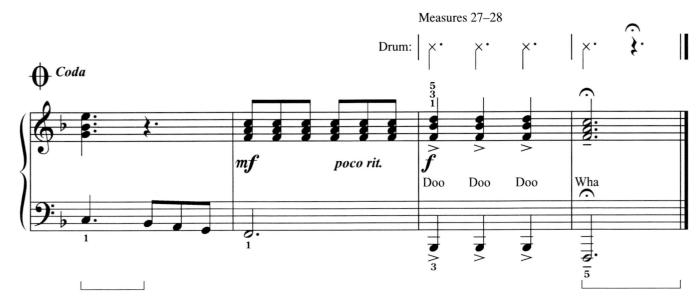

For my student Natsuki (Nacky) Mase:
I hope that you will always love and enjoy the piano.

SPICY SALSA

Optional Percussion:
Measures 1–25

Catherine Rollin

With spirit and spunk

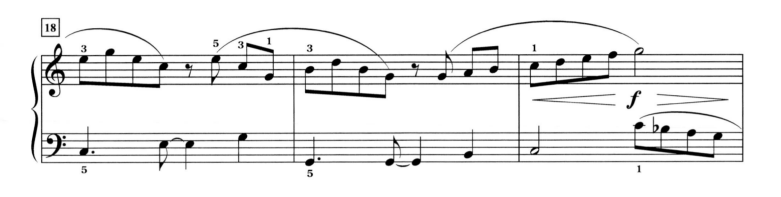

Measure 26

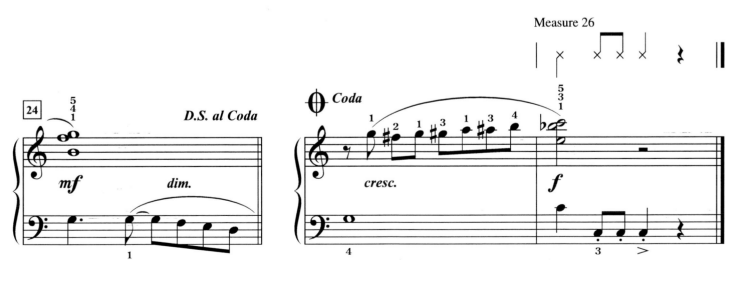

For Christine Dubov and the late Stephen Dubov who inspired
and touched the souls of many through music and dance.

MEDITERRANEAN DANCE

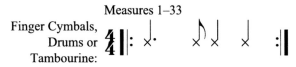

Catherine Rollin

Winding moderately—very legato and expressive

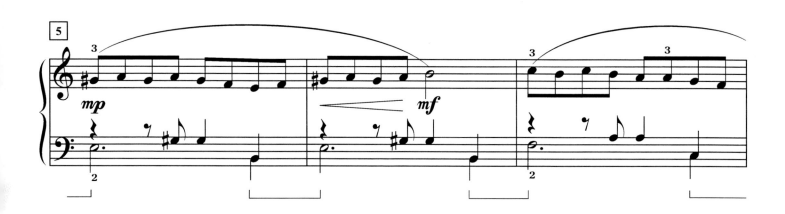

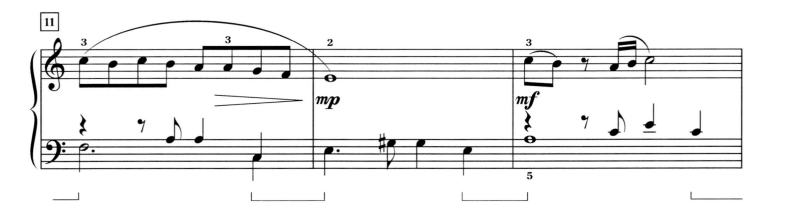

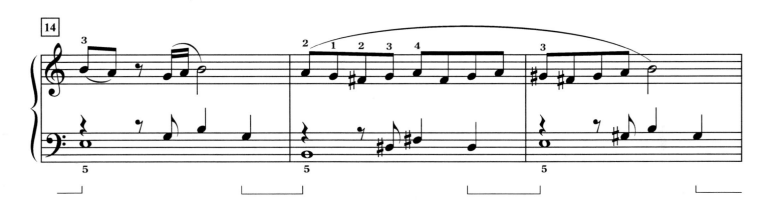

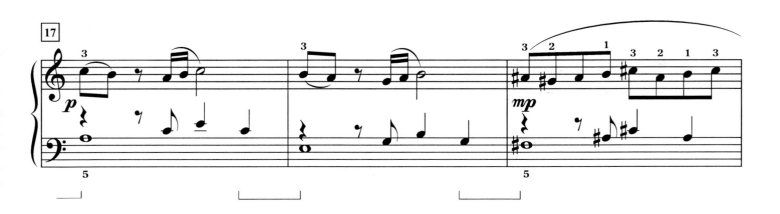

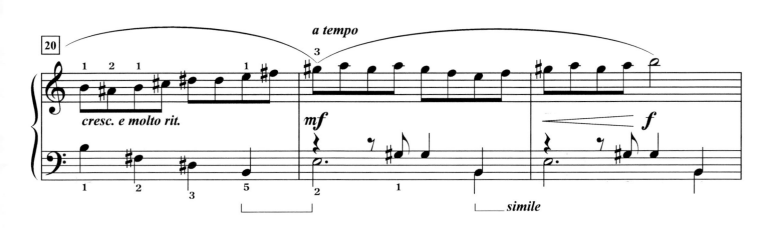

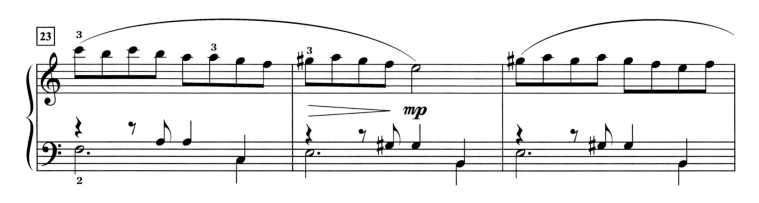

Measure 34

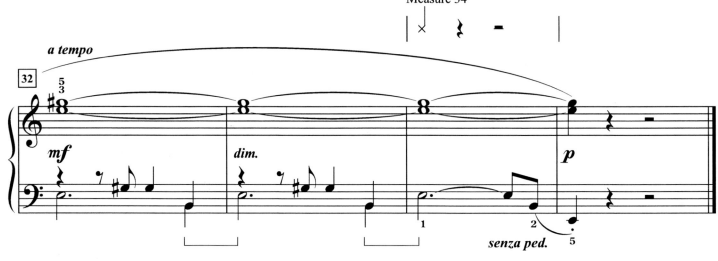

For the piano teachers in Hiroshima, Japan:
Thank you for your warm welcome and your dedication to piano teaching.

MAKE MINE CHA-CHA-CHA!

Catherine Rollin

* Play all staccatos with a slightly detached portato touch.

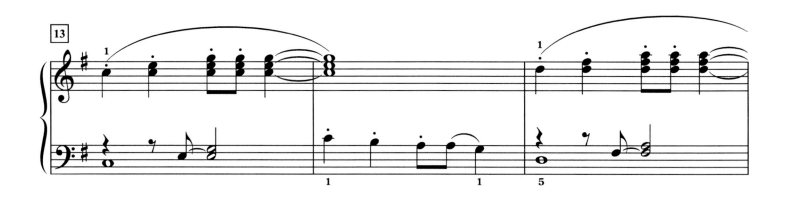

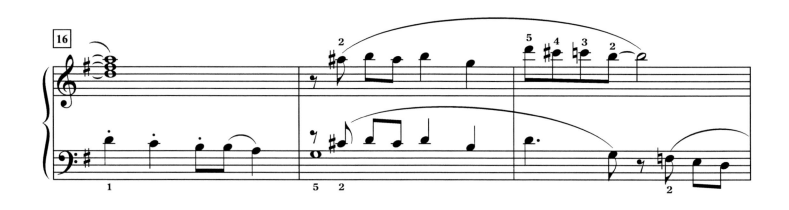

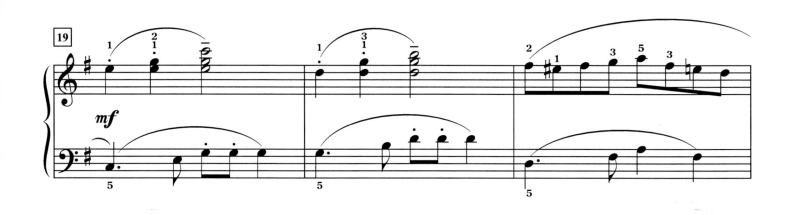

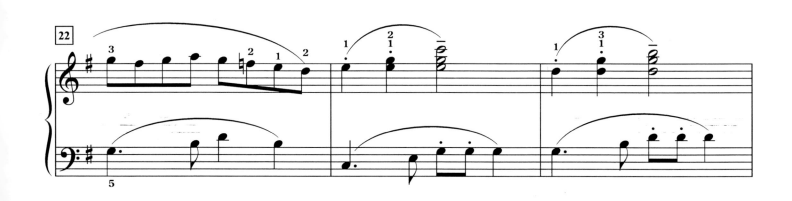

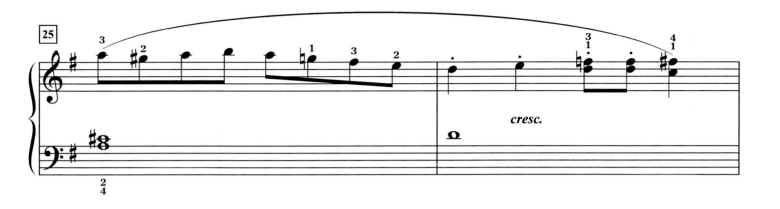

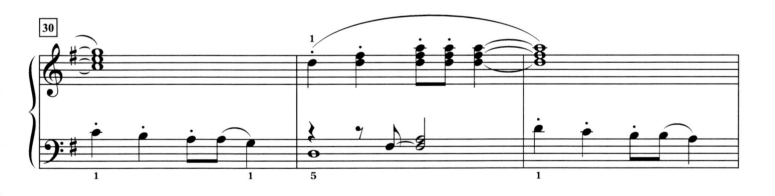

Measure 34

Drums & Maracas:

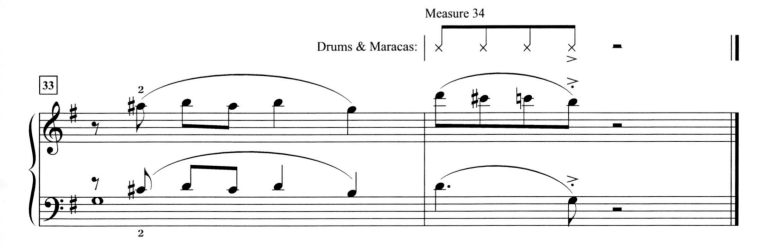